TO HAVE AND TO HOLD

OTHER RELATED TITLES
FROM SOLID GROUND

In addition to the book *To Have and To Hold* Solid Ground has several significant titles for the Christian Family, including:

The Secret of Happy Home Life by J.R. Miller
"This is one of the most helpful and heartwarming books I have read on family relationships. Though written a hundred years ago, its message is timeless and much needed today." – Jerry Bridges

Sermons for Christian Families by Edward Payson
"This is Edward Payson at his best--full of wisdom and practicality. As parents, read these sermons for your own edification, then read them aloud with passion to your teenagers and older children." - Dr. Joel R. Beeke

Stepping Heavenward by Elizabeth Prentiss
"This book is a treasure of both godly and womanly wisdom told with disarming candor and humility, yet revealing a deep heart's desire to know God." – Elisabeth Elliott

Mothers of the Wise and Good by Jabez Burns
"This book answers the very questions that today's women are asking. The engaging anecdotes and instructive essays are wonderful. I have looked for a book like this for many years. Every mother, grandmother, and spiritual mother - in others words, every woman - will find great help and hope in this book." - Susan Hunt

The Excellent Woman by Anne Pratt
"This is a work that will bear to be read more than once, and each successive reading wiil be likely to reveal some new gem of thought. It is a book suitable for the husband to present to his wife, the mother to her daughter, and the brother to his sister; and the more widely it is circulated, the better for the country and the world." – W.B. Sprague

The Mother at Home by John Abbott
"Christian mothers who want biblical counsel on Christian child rearing will find this book valuable." -Grace and Truth Books

The Child at Home by John Abbott
"This book powerfully cultivates within children's consciences the need to honor God and their parents by promoting the need for heartfelt obedience, religious truth, genuine piety, biblical character traits, a sense of responsibility, and a dread of deception." – Joel Beeke

The Family at Home by Gorham Abbott
The Family at Home contains 68 practical chapters covering everything from courtship and marriage to showing respect for the aged. These chapters are brief but filled with wise and godly advice for the entire family.

Call us at 205-443-0311
Visit us on-line at www.solid-ground-books.com

TO HAVE AND TO HOLD

A
CHRISTIAN MINISTER'S
AFFECTIONATE ADVICE
TO
A MARRIED COUPLE

Rev. James Bean

Including a letter
from the
Rev. Henry Venn, A.M.

Originally
Published by the
American Tract Society,
28 Cornhill, Boston

Solid Ground Christian Books
Birmingham, Alabama USA

Solid Ground Christian Books
PO Box 660132
Vestavia Hills AL 35266
205-443-0311
mike.sgcb@gmail.com
www.solid-ground-books.com

TO HAVE AND TO HOLD
A Christian Minister's Affectionate Advice to a Married Couple
by Rev. James Bean

First Solid Ground Edition March 2010

Taken from the 19th century edition published by
the American Tract Society, New York, NY

Cover photo is of the wedding of John Joseph Strunk
and Rachel Elizabeth Gaydosh on July 23, 1999,
in Merrick, Long Island, New York.

Cover design by Borgo Design, Tuscaloosa, AL

ISBN: 978-159925-148-6

CONTENTS

The Marriage Vow
Wedding Gifts
Epithalamuim
Bridal Union
Heavenly Love
True Affection
Human Bliss
Matrimony
Empire of Woman
Speak Kindly
Equality
The True Heart's Aspirations

Advice
to
A Married Couple

CHAPTER I

Important Nature of the Married Union.—
Danger of Remissness in Duties Formerly Paid.—
Treatment of Relations.

As the minister of a benevolent religion, it is
not enough for me to have joined your hands
together at the altar. It becomes me to follow
you from thence with my earnest prayers, that
you may long enjoy together every comfort
implied in the solemn benediction lately
pronounced over you. Let me now add a few
useful considerations, with respect to the
relation into which you have entered.

The marriage relationship is the most important of any you are capable of forming in this life. It is not your own happiness only, but that of others also, that may be affected by an improper behavior in this connection. It is a union constituted with a view not merely to the reciprocal benefit of the two persons who agree to form it, but likewise to the manners and the happiness of society at large.

Smaller communities are the nurseries of larger ones. At a certain time of life a transplantation is made, and the larger field of society takes it character from those qualities which were brought into it from the little enclosures of family life. You are therefore not to consider yourselves merely as two friends who have agreed to share each other's trials or enjoyments, but as the founders of a little community of rational and immortal creatures, who may hereafter found other small communities, and from whom, in process of time, a *multitude* may spring. To this multitude, stationed here and there according to the allotments of divine Providence, you may give a cast of character, the influence of which may be matter of pleasure or of pain, both to themselves and those with whom they are connected, long after you have ceased to act in the present scene. And though you may never move far from the spot on which these observations are addressed to you,—yea, and ere long be forgotten even in this little circle,—yet the good or evil influence of your conduct on this circumscribed spot may take such a range as to be felt where the name even of your country is scarcely known.

But even this, though a large view of the possible extent of your influence is comparatively but a confined one. It may be felt to eternity. The members of your family are *immortals*. Such also will be their successors. They will not only have a place in society, but an account to render to GOD. Before him they must appear at the great audit of the world, *"to receive according to the things done in the body, whether they be good or bad,"* (2 Cor. 5:10) and to you they may be in some measure indebted for the terror or the transport they may feel at that solemn hour.

From these considerations, see the *importance* of your marital connection, and accept of that advice which your minister feels it his duty to address to you.

I will consider you as *fellow-travelers* on the road of life; not brought together by accident, or as those who have consented to keep together on the journey merely from a regard to convenience, but from a cordial esteem of each other, heightened by a tender attachment, which has led you to make choice of each other as companions, independent of a view to the conveniences of traveling in company. You have given yourselves up to each other, and have, in the presence of GOD, pledged yourselves to bear each other's burdens, to consult each other's peace of mind, and to concur invariably in endeavoring to render the journey as pleasant to each other as possible. Thus conjoined, you have committed a trust to each other. Neither of you have your felicity in your own hands. Neither of you have it in your power to be completely happy without the consent of the other. Never may you repent of this surrender! But a knowledge of the imperfections of human nature makes me anxious for you, lest, after rendering the first stage of the journey delightful by the interchange of every endearment, you should sink into the unhappy condition of those who the greatest infelicity of the journey is, that they are obligated to travel together.

To avoid the evils into which the infirmities of our nature may plunge us, we should enter presently on the use of preventives.

With this view, *the first thing* to which I exhort you is *an attention to the preservation of that affection for each other* which first determined you to be partners for life. In the continuance of this alone, you will find the sufferings of the present state considerably reduced. Trials and difficulties are the common lot of humanity, and you cannot hope for an exemption from them. Rough roads, dark

To Have and to Hold

nights, and stormy days, are to be expected; but while your affections continue undiminished, you will, in this circumstance, find a considerable alleviation of the difficulties with which you have to contend. The trials which occur by the way will be less felt when they serve as occasions of providing afresh the care and tenderness which the travelers here have for each other.

When I exhort you to attend to the preservation of that affection which first determined you to become partners for life, I am not to be understood as if I expected that the fervor experienced at its commencement would continue. No; I would apprize you that ere long *that* will abate. But, though time and familiarity will assuredly carry off much of the first ardor, a true affection will receive improvement from time. Time will render it a more chastened, rational, and steady principle, if it be cultivated. If it be cultivated, I say; otherwise there may be a transition from idolatry to aversion.

To cultivate this kind of affection, neither of you should be remiss in those attentions which you have been accustomed to pay to each other. Let not the husband grow negligent of any of those marks of regard by which a wife feels herself acknowledged preeminently as a friend and companion. She perceives herself *still* distinguished when all the esteem, compassion, or good manners which her partner is ready to express to others is, with a promptitude evidently unstudied, still more cordially shown to her. Conjugal affection is a delicate plant. It cannot thrive under indifference. Sullen silence checks its growth. But it dies when scarcely any time is spent at home; when everybody can interest the husband in conversation but the wife; when she is the last person thought of in a recreation, or the least considered in an accommodation. None but an idiot can support that sort of treatment, by which a wife sees herself rated merely as a kind of domestic animal.

Let not, however, the wife be too ready to consider the behavior of her husband as expressive of indifference. Such conclusions often originate in the folly, pride, or petulance of the observer. To prevent our drawing them too hastily, let it be considered that, as an object becomes familiar to us, our esteem of it, though not diminished, naturally becomes a more silent sentiment. A woman must guard against the tormenting disappointments to which childish expectations render her liable. For there is a childishness in her expecting always to be caressed; and, if she does not become more rational in her expectations, this folly will occasion its own punishment. She will fancy that she is neglected; she will complain; and her complaints will produce aversion.

There should likewise be some allowance made for what is natural to men, especially Englishmen—namely, a certain bluntness, through which they seem to be indifferent when they are not really so. What may seem to improper judges inattention to others, to more penetrating observers is manifestly nothing but an honest inattention to themselves; a superiority to the mean arts of those interested persons whose chief study is the cultivation of a pleasing address.

But should there appear at times something more than mere inattention, something that evidences a disturbance of temper, she is then perhaps called to allow for the agitations of mind to which *men* are particularly liable, from their having more to do with the world than women have.[1] It is a serene region in which a woman moves; not so that into which the head of a family is often driven for the support of those who depend on him. In the midst of a thousand vexations from the stupidity, negligence, or knavery of those with whom his business lays, he has to earn that bread which his wife and children may eat in tranquility. Should he, therefore, when he comes home from this turbulent scene, omit a customary

---

[1] Rev. Bean wrote these words at a time that women very seldom left the confines of the home to work outside. Sadly, this is no longer the case. Multitudes of women seek their fulfillment outside the home, even after having children. Gladly, many families are beginning to rethink the wisdom of this practice and are returning to the old way.

mark of affection, eat his meal in silence, or return a short answer to a civil question, let not the wife consider such behavior as any proof of indifference to her. Let her not listen to that *demon of discord* who would prompt her to resent it as such. Let her recollect that now is the time for her to exert the peculiar virtues of her sex; to call forth all the sweetness, humanity, and tenderness of her nature, in order to soothe him who has been toiling all the day, principally, perhaps, with a view to her comfort.

In cautioning a wife not to be too ready to consider herself neglected, I have not imparted the whole of my advice to her. I have admonished the husband not to be negligent of those marks of regard which are due to his partner; and she is to remember that the same duty is incumbent on her. It will be impossible for affection to be preserved, if she tread in the steps of those inconsiderate persons, who as soon as the marriage rites are celebrated, become remiss in certain engaging things, of which they before had been scrupulously observant. Must not she sink in the esteem of any understanding man, who by her conduct seems to say, "I have now obtained my settlement"? And nothing is more calculated to suggest such an idea than a relaxation of former attention. When a woman abandons herself to sloth and indulgence; when she degenerates from neatness to negligence, from industry to indolence, from kindness to selfishness; when these omissions are continued without any necessary cause, after they been gently remonstrated against,—it is natural for a man of reflection to read this sordid sentiment in his wife's bosom, and for a man of generosity to recoil at the discovery.

She who dreads the entertainment of such an opinion of her in the mind of her husband must take care to let it have no support from her conduct. She knows what is now pleasing to him, by remembering what was *formerly* so. And he knows how capable she is of giving him pleasure, by recollecting the methods she once took for this purpose, and that they are still practicable. If, with the power still in her hands, she is remiss in the act, there is but one inference for him to make—namely, that it is a matter about which she is not as solicitous as she once was.

Here I am naturally led to notice a monstrous perversion of character observed in some of the sex. I have seen a woman negligent of all the duties that are peculiar to her, and yet tormentingly busy in her husband's immediate province. If a woman would preserve the affections of her husband, let her not only be attentive to him in all the engaging actions which her sex, her situation in the family, and her vows, give him a right to expect from her, but let her *confine* herself to these.

The disposal of his time, or his property, his journeys, his connections, &c., are things to be regulated by the circumstances of his calling — a subject which he probably best understands. I cannot but advise her, therefore, for her own sake as well as his, to leave these things entirely to his management, and to remember that it is her province to soften, to cheer, and to refresh that mind on which the weightiest cares of a family press.

The unfriendly tendency of such inter- ference in women to the maintenance of mutual affection is, however, not more manifest than is that of a supercilious treatment of women. I refer to those ungracious men who never honor the understanding, or contribute to the satisfaction of a wife. For, though not able to dictate, may she not be capable of advising? Many a man, wise in his own esteem, might have been saved from ruin, had he only deliberated with that prudent, thoughtful, and affectionate wife, to whose inquiries he would scarcely vouchsafe an answer, though introduced with all the graces by which a gentle and submissive spirit solicits attention.

Far be this supercilious behavior from him to whom I address these precautions, and who has solemnly pledged himself, not only to maintain, but to *honor* his wife. Rather let him deliberate with her who ought to be his dearest, and is his most disinterested friend—even in those affairs which it is his immediate duty to superintend. He may derive useful hints from a female mind in some particulars, though it may not, from want of practice, be comprehensive enough to grasp the whole of his system. And if not, yet he gratifies an innocent solicitude to know something of affairs in which she is interested. At least, he prevents the mortification which a sullen or contemptuous concealment occasions.

Such communications contribute very much to keep up the warmth of a rational affection, as they honor the understanding of a woman; as they give her credit for taking an equal interest with her husband in his cares, anxieties, and labors; and above all, as in such deliberations she feels herself treated as a friend. There is a way of conducting them which draws after it nothing to regret. It will be for the happiness of both parties that these communications be obviously the issues of a generous confidence.

There is a circumstance in every matrimonial connection which may have a considerable influence on the happiness of a married pair: there are *relations* on both sides. On properly managing the regard paid to these persons, the preservation of mutual affections is found in many cases very much to depend.

Here some of the most humiliating instances have been exhibited of that selfishness which cannot be satisfied with anything short of the monopoly of affection. How unreasonable is it to expect that love to me should extinguish affections which are due to those whom duty, nature, and habit require me *yet* to love! Our mind is perverted, if we do not perceive something additionally amiable in that married person, who, in the midst of new connections, cares, and occupations, still shows to a tender parent the affectionate and reverential spirit of a dutiful child, or manifests the still existing union of souls which interested a fond brother and sister in each other's happiness. If my affections be rational, they will be heightened by observing that the object of my peculiar attachment appears amiable, in whatever relation I view this object. On the other hand, I am the subject of a sordid passion, if I can rest satisfied with attentions paid to me, while I observe that the person thus devoted to me is inattentive to everything and everyone else.

Affection to our kindred is not inconsistent with the fondest attachment of the heart to a husband or a wife. Do not, therefore, encourage that littleness and pride which would lead you to think yourself defrauded of something that was your own, when you see any tender regard paid to them. It is a mean jealousy of temper that makes us *prompt* to consider ourselves rivaled. It is a base pride that leads us to put an invidious construction on those signs of respect and esteem which are shown to others. Let married persons guard against such a cause of unhappiness to themselves, by considering that the distribution of affection does not necessarily diminish its quantity, but that it is even capable of increasing as the objects on which it is exercised multiply. Conjugal affection can indeed be shared by only two persons; but this may grow and strengthen without any loss sustained to it from the cultivation of filial or fraternal affection.

While the bonds of matrimony must not be suffered to dissolve those of filial piety, it may be as well, however, to suggest this to married persons: *Let them avoid, as far as is consistent with duty to relations, that kind of manner, in their treatment of them, which is calculated to awaken jealousy in the married partner.* Through neglect of this rule of prudence, the visit of a relation has sometimes been the period of misery to a couple who have hitherto lived in harmony. Can we not be glad to see a parent, a sister, or a brother, without reducing a wife or a husband to a cipher[2] in the house during their stay in it? Is it prudent to be so profuse in the expressions of our regard for them as to lead the partner of our life to have an interest in their departure?

These admonitions on the article of attentions seemed to me deserving of your regard. That matrimony was instituted for the

---

[2] Cipher - One having no influence or value; a nonentity.

happiness of mankind there can be no doubt. But it is not necessary to the fulfillment of this intention that happiness should spring up spontaneously to those who enter into the marriage state. It deserves our thankfulness to Him who ordained this union, that it will fully answer its intention to those who will be at the pains of guarding against whatever may defeat that intention.

By this sober view I wish you to adjust your hopes. Do not entertain expectations of bliss which the circumstances of the world, and the foolishness of your nature, will render it impossible to realize. You must not only expect to meet with untoward circumstances in the world, but likewise to discover faults in each other. Neither the scene nor the actors will be found to answer the ideas you may have formed of them. The scene you cannot alter; it will be managed by a superior power; but you may accommodate yourselves to it. And this is incumbent on you, not only in the relation you both sustain to the great Disposer, but with respect to the obligations you are under to support one another comfortably, in the various changes through which you may have to pass.

Among other things which should be your care in this view is the cultivation of *good temper*. But to the consideration of so essential a point I shall appropriate a separate chapter.

CHAPTER II

Importance of a Kind and
Amiable Temper and Deportment.

Without a good temper you can neither enjoy a pleasing situation nor support an inconvenient one. Without good nature there may be many valuable qualities; but they would be all gladly exchanged for that sweetness of disposition which compensates for a thousand defects. With this engaging quality, the attentions which have been recommended will be so far from being impracticable that they will be, as it were, spontaneously produced; or, if there be an occasional failure, the omission will be kindly interpreted. It will be attributed to want of thought, rather than to any thing of a more reprehensible nature.

The improvement of our temper is a thing not so much out of our power as is commonly supposed. The general idea is that good temper is a certain gift of nature, like beauty, which a man can not have unless he is born with it. It must be confessed that some seem formed, from their very birth, to be the delight of the human kind in this respect, and that others, again, seem to have brought into the world with them an unhappiness of temper which seems incapable of improvement. The generality of mankind, however, are not found in these extremes. The temper of most people is made up of a mixture of good and bad. The character of the person, in point of temper, is denominated from that quality which has the ascendency.

The predominance of a condemnable temper is not to be charged wholly to the circumstances that excite it, but in part to the not imposing on ourselves that discipline which counteracts the influence of those circumstances which tend to deprave the temper. That the good in our temper must prevail is a most desirable thing; and this desirable thing is attainable. Now, if interest may be allowed to second the voice of duty, hear what it says to the wedded pair: "If you wish to render your union delightful in all situations, and to relish it to the very last, seek the improvement of your temper at any price."

On the cultivation of good nature let me suggest a few hints.

Endeavor to ascertain what is that particular defect of temper into which you are most liable to fall, and make a point of setting a strong guard over yourself in that particular. Let this idea be ever present to your mind: "At that weak part of my nature all the miseries of matrimonial life may enter." This will probably be found a hard service; but the necessity of the case obliges you to it. You have the choice of but two things: you must be incessantly vigilant and self-denying here, or suffer every domestic delight to be torn from you.

But I have another piece of advice to give—namely, Avoid the *occasions* which excite any unruly temper to which you may be liable. This advice is given to you both, with respect to each other. Having ascertained each other's particular imperfection, you have likewise learned what things they are that call it forth. That which provokes your partner must, as far as possible, be shunned.

Here a number of *little things* become objects deserving attention. Nor must they be passed over because they are little. Little things are felt to have great power when they act upon a tender part. An insect could have blinded Samson when in his full strength. No small portion of the uneasiness that has embittered married life has arisen out of the insect occurrences which every day produces; and, contemptible as they are in themselves, they must be watched on account of the mischief of which they are capable.

There is no evil which petty occurrences more frequently generate than *disputes;* nor are there many things which it is more the interest of the married pair to guard against. "The contentions of a wife," says Solomon, "are a continual dripping." Drop after drop wears a deeper impression than a thousand storms. What, therefore, is that unthinking woman about who indulges a disputing spirit; who will debate *every* point, and have the last word about straws? She is forcing her husband into other society, and that, perhaps, to which he has had many objections, all of which, however, are at length overcome by the refuge it affords him from the misery of incessant debate. It is not, perhaps, so much to the commission of the more alarming crimes, as to the frequency of frivolous disputes, that the alienation of married people from each other is to be generally ascribed. I may add that in these irritating encounters deeds of the worst kind have often had their beginning. Whatever, therefore, you forget, let me conjure[3] both of you to remember the mischief of frivolous disputes.

After all your care, perhaps, some occasional effects of your respective weaknesses will occur. Yet it is not a few eruptions of this sort that will throw you back in the cultivation of good nature, if you can learn to

---

[3] Conjure - to appeal earnestly or strongly to

make due allowance for *constitutional infirmity* in each other. Attend, therefore, to this plain lesson. It will have its advantage in suppressing an unhappy temper in many instances. Where there is a readiness to make this wise and humane allowance, the heart will be no more alienated by a little sally of temper than by a fit of epilepsy. The paroxysm, in either case, will call forth the compassion of the spectator.

Be it remembered, however, that we must not be called upon too frequently for this allowance, and that it will hardly ever be granted, unless the *tenor* of life be such as forbids a severe construction of an occasional failure. It is, indeed, the tenor of life that preserves or destroys affections. It is not a few brilliant expressions of love, in the midst of constant unkindness, that will make us enjoy the marriage union; nor is it a few deviations from the line of duty that will render it unpleasant, while the general course of life is expressive of kindness and unquestionable affection. Make a point, therefore, of disciplining your own temper; and be assured that by so doing the connection which you have formed will be more than tolerable: it will be pleasing. The recollection of it at some period distant from its commencement will be grateful; notwithstanding there may be some things that occur to you, in this retrospect, which you will wish had been otherwise.

Let me entreat you to bestow all the pains on this point which it may require. What equivalent can be found for good nature? Let the husband be sober and industrious; let the wife be chaste and frugal: by these virtues you may be preserved from some of the miseries which wait on profligacy and extravagance; but, while you escape these, what will your house be without good nature? Not a home. By a *home* we understand a place in which the mind can settle; where it is too much at ease to be inclined to rove; a refuge to which we flee in the expectation of finding those calm pleasures, those soothing kindnesses, which are the sweetness of life.

All the admonitions, therefore, that I might detail on the article of temper, may be comprised in this short precept: *Endeavor to make your house a home to each other.* Absence will then be no gratification to either party. By the husband's attending to this precept, his return will be welcomed by those whom he left at home. By the wife's observance of this maxim, the husband will return with a pleasure equal to that with which he is received. "The heart of her husband doth safely trust in her." Over the door of his house he will see written, "SACRED TO PEACE;" thither, in the assurance of enjoying that repose he cannot find in the world, he will hasten from its toils and vexations.

CHAPTER III

Influence of Christian Piety on the Happiness of Married Life. —Conduct Which the Holy Scriptures Require in Married Persons Toward Each Other.

The observations which I now proceed to make are of the utmost consequence. Were I to omit them, I should put into your hands a very imperfect directory for your conduct in that state of life, on which you have now entered. I have reserved the important subject now to be introduced for the latter part of my address; for I wish, above all things, to leave the impression of this on your minds at our parting.

Whatever be our situation, there is one thing indispensably necessary to our enjoyment of the happiness it is capable of yielding: *we must endeavor to acquit ourselves as the servants of GOD in that situation.* Thereby we obtain his blessing in it; without which no condition can long be either safe or comfortable. Let the situation be social or commercial; let it promise little or much; let the government of an empire or only the care of a family be committed to us,—the observation holds equally true. The lot lies in this world, concerning which GOD has said to mankind, "Thorns and briers shall it bring forth unto you." Piety, however, has resources in a world lying under such a sentence. I persuade myself that you mean to adopt the rules I have suggested to you; yet I should not expect them to be long followed, if I doubted of your having the fear of GOD in your heart.

Nor is there, if this be wanting, any good security for continued happiness, even in those marriage connections where the parties have joined their hands from the most sincere affection for each other. Without this, the sources of patience, resignation, forbearance, compassion, and candid allowance for natural infirmity, are small, and may be soon exhausted. Nor can it be expected that we shall persevere in the more arduous part of that kind of self-discipline which has been mentioned, if reverence for the will of GOD, and an earnest desire to please him in all things, are wanting. If, therefore, you have rushed into this connection regardless of what is incumbent on you as immortal beings, your business is to correct this error. Its influence will otherwise run through the whole web of life, and prevent many of those enjoyments which marriage was designed to bestow on mankind.

If, however, you are persons of genuine religion, this circumstance is a most favorable omen of your future life. It is the smile of heaven. The maintenance of mutual affection has been recommended to you as a great object of the attention of a married couple. And what is so likely to keep up its vigor as a deeply-rooted regard to a religion which cherishes all the tenderness of which our nature is capable? Such is Christianity—a religion which exhibits the highest example of benevolence, and suggests the most powerful motives to its imitation.

Christian piety promises to keep the spirit of conjugal affection alive by that sublime species of benevolence which induces an earnest desire for the spiritual and eternal welfare of all, but especially of those to whom we are more nearly allied. And it has likewise always at hand a motive to the exercise of forgiveness, by that sense of *our own faults,* and our consequent need of forgiveness from GOD, with which it is ever accompanied.

Religion, while it thus calls forth and strengthens the mutual tenderness of those allied in marriage, further provides for their continued happiness by teaching them not to expect too much from each other, since neither of them has married an angel, but a human being, "compassed with infirmity." This just view makes them sober in their expectations, and does much to perpetuate their enjoyment.

Actuated by religions principles, the married pair will not have their happiness interrupted by those altercations which are produced between the love of pleasure and the necessity of resisting its continual and excessive demands. They will likewise be preserved from the embarrassments which in the end embitter this connection where the parties have agreed in adopting an expensive style of living. In short, it is by these, and many other concomitants of genuine piety, that old age steals on without bringing with it the misery of feeling that there is nothing left but the dregs of worn-out enjoyments; something yet remains that can be tasted without exciting disgust.

Mistake me not, as if by piety I meant merely the making a profession of religion; or the adoption of that system of truths you hear from me your minister. There are people who go thus far, and yet afford as affecting instances of the unhappiness of married life as any. Christian piety must have, like many other things, its principles; and the more truth there be in the principles, the more purity and energy there is likely to be in the practice. But the mere adoption of opinions, however sound, is not

Christian piety. This is a thing that is manifested by making the word of GOD the rule of life.

A truly pious man makes the Holy Scriptures the rule both of his expectations and his conduct. Making them the rule of his expectations, he embraces "the faith once delivered to the saints," whatever reception it may have in that age in which he happens to live; making them the rule of his conduct, he consults them with respect to the several relations he may sustain in life, that he may "know how he ought to walk and please GOD." GOD has given very particular directions how to conduct ourselves in relative life that in situations of such importance the servant of GOD may not be at a loss how to act. The married person, particularly, has his behavior marked out; and these passages the man of piety will study.

The superficial religionist will not, indeed be thus attentive to the preceptive part of Scripture. It is lamentable to observe how many there are who take up the volume of inspiration merely as a book that discovers an expedient for escaping punishment, never regarding it as the directory of conduct. If these are your models, you will neither adorn nor enjoy the religion you profess. There is nothing to be expected from your religion, unless it be of that genuine kind which will make each of you attentive, as in the sight of GOD, to your respective duties.

What I have, therefore, to recommend to you is, serious meditation, accompanied with prayer to GOD, on those passages of Scripture which teach you how to act in this relation. They were rehearsed to you when your nuptials were solemnized. And as part of an inspired book, you are to consider the exhortation in the office of matrimony, as GOD'S charge to you from the altar.

"Husbands, *love* your wives, even as Christ also loved the church, and gave himself for it, that he might sanctify and cleanse it with the washing of water by the word, that he might present it to himself a glorious church, not having spot, or wrinkle, or any such thing, but that it should be holy, and without blemish. So ought men to love their wives as their own bodies. Let everyone so love his wife, even as himself." (Eph. 5: 25-33.) "Husbands, love your wives, and *be not bitter against them.*" (Col. 3:19.) "Ye husbands, *give honor* unto the wife, as unto the weaker vessel." (1 Pet. 3:7.)

Perhaps no part of Scripture less requires a comment. To understand the meaning of familiar terms is all that is necessary. The Christian Husband is taught by this passage that GOD requires him to love the woman he has chosen; to be kind and tender to her; yea, to honor her; and, therefore, that the domestic tyrant, the fierce animadverter[4] on every little omission, the husband whose contemptuous treatment of a wife is an habitual degradation of her, are persons condemned by the Lord of all; who is to be considered as the Avenger of the wrongs of every deserving wife thus injured. Here husbands may learn that something more is required of them than merely to afford a maintenance[5] to a wife. Nothing can compensate for the lack of that love required in the passage above quoted. What is a maintenance, any further than it is enjoyed? and how impossible is this, unless it is accompanied with tenderness, kindness, and respectful treatment in words and actions. Alas! for want of these endearments, many a woman, who by her dress seems to tell the world she has a husband that spares no expense to gratify her, is in all her finery, to be considered as a gaudy victim, ever bleeding under the hands of domestic cruelty. She is as little to be envied as the devoted animal which stood at the altar of sacrifice ornamented with a wreath of flowers.

All that the warmest advocate for women can enforce on husbands being expressly required by GOD himself, as the passages previously quoted show, the next thing to be

---

[4] One who animadverts; a censurer; also [Obs.], a chastiser.

[5] Providing a maintenance is simply earning money enough to provide for the basic needs of the family.

considered is the *example* which the inspired writer has selected for the model of a husband's behavior toward his companion. "Husbands, love your wives, *even as Christ loved the church, and gave himself for it,* that he might sanctify and cleanse it with the washing of water by the word; that he might present it to himself a glorious church, not having spot or wrinkle, or any such thing." (Eph. 5:25-27.)

Here is at once *example* and *motive.* What more could even an inspired man say, in order to form the husband to everything affectionate, disinterested, sympathizing, and attentive to his wife, than this: *"Love her as Christ loved the church?"* He who understands Christianity finds a volume in such a sentence. His mind instantly recurs to that astonishing instance of benevolence which his Redeemer exhibited, in giving himself up to sufferings and death for our salvation; to that which he showed in sending forth ministers to "preach the gospel to every creature;" to the tender attention which he pays, now he is in heaven, to all who receive this gospel, taking care that everything be provided which is necessary to increase their faith, purify their hearts, administer to their conflicts, and cherish the hope which he has formed in them of participating in the fulfillment of those gracious purposes toward his church which are to be consummated in heaven and enjoyed to all eternity. This, says he, is my *pattern.* Such a friend as Christ was to his church am I to be to my spouse. Am I a part of that body of which he is such a Savior? Then he gave himself for *me.* Let me imitate that affection, of the fruits of which I humbly hope I am a partaker. I here find myself required to love my wife, though she is not without fault; to interpose between her and danger; to supply, as far as in my power, everything which can contribute to her comfort; to seek not only her present, but her everlasting happiness; for thus did Christ love his church.

To the wife the Word of GOD speaks thus: "Wives, *submit* yourselves unto your own husbands, as unto the Lord. For the husband is the head of the wife, even as Christ is the head of the church. Therefore, as the church is *subject* unto Christ, so let the wives be to their own husbands, in everything." (Eph. 5: 22-24.) "Let the wife see that she reverence her husband." (Eph. 5:33.)

Here we should particularly notice that virtue on which the admonition principally turns—namely, submission. A virtue so prominently commended ought certainly to be considered, as meriting particular attention.

It need not surely be necessary to observe that the superiority which the Scriptures give to the man over the woman is *not* that of a master over a slave. The precepts enforced on the husband are of such a kind as to show that the superiority with which he is invested is founded in reason and maintained by love. GOD has not required from the woman the submission of a slave, but a reasonable and advantageous submission, such as a man of good sense knows it becomes him to receive, and an affectionate wife will yield with pleasure. Some women, however, consider everything of this kind as the relinquishing of all self-defense. Mistaken creatures! It is their best security, as well as one of their loveliest ornaments: (1 Pet. 3:4) like polished armor, it is both beauty and defense.

Considering the importance given to the virtue now under consideration, we see at a glance how far from that character which the Holy Scriptures recommend to women are those who deny to a husband any rule in his house unless he purchase it at the expense of peace. Such conduct is against not only the spirit, but the very letter, of Christianity: "Let wives be subject to their own husbands *in everything.*"

The apostle, as if to prevent the possibility of a misunderstanding, enforces his point by a most striking illustration: "Wives, submit yourselves unto your own husbands, as unto the Lord. For the husband is the head of the wife, even as Christ is the head of the church; and he is the Savior of the body. *Therefore, as the church is subject unto Christ, so let the wives be to their own husband* in everything" (Eph. 5:22-24).

The church is subject to Christ to this extent. She is always to be known by these circumstances: that as her Legislator, she receives laws from Christ; as her Lord, she receives commands from him; as her Guide, she follows him. That religious society, therefore, which renounces the authority of Christ, and sets up for its own directress in matters of faith and morals, is not the church. Nor is any individual, who may be thus characterized, to be considered as a part of the Church of Christ; "which is the blessed company of all faithful people."[6]

This model of subjection, unreserved subordination, and reverential deference, is a woman in the ties of wedlock to make her *exemplar,* if she would be found in that relation such as GOD approves. Let her be frugal, industrious, cleanly, and chaste; she is to have the praise of all these good qualities; but let her remember that, if withal she is self-willed and refractory, she is destitute of that virtue in which the Holy Scriptures seem to have concentrated all the good qualities of a wife. Much as she may triumph in the contemplation of her superiority over the idle and extravagant with whom she compares herself, she resists the order of GOD; and she resembles not the church, but the *world.* She

---

[6] These words are taken from the Book of Common Prayer.

acts as if she were determined to go as far as possible from the pattern which GOD has set before her, and had chosen one that is the very reverse of the church. Such is the world; in all points, an affecting contrast to the spouse of Christ: rebelling against the government, to which his spouse most gladly yields herself; despising that authority, which she loves to honor; and with equal ingratitude and folly, rising up against the power, which both her obligations and her interest require her to obey.

Let the husband and the wife contemplate the two examples which an inspired apostle has chosen for their respective imitation, and they will find that all which has been said in the former part of this address is bound on them from more authoritative considerations: *GOD himself requires it of them.*

Make a point of sitting down to reflect on these and other passages in the Sacred Writings, in which the duties of husband and wife are set forth. Perhaps, if you made it a rule at the return of any particular day—the annual return of your wedding day, for instance—to peruse them, it might prevent your entirely overlooking what so much concerns the credit and the comfort of each other.

Let me request you both to charge yourselves with this task. Attend to what GOD teaches you on the subject; and reject, with indignation, those opposite sentiments with which the careless and profligate part of mankind daily insult both GOD and man. I would have you not only *read* the passages of Scripture, but examine yourselves by them. "Am I this kind of person in this relation? Did I act in such a thing agreeably to the spirit of these words?" Should any unpleasant circumstances in future arise, inquire whether they may or may not be attributed to your departure from the pattern set before you. In thus examining yourselves by the appointed rule of duty, you may discover what there is in your particular constitution to render the imitation of the pattern peculiarly difficult to you. Carry such difficulties to GOD, not to request him to relax his laws but to obtain from him those extraordinary succors which you may need, in order to act on all occasions worthy of your Christian profession.

These are the marks of genuine religion, a divine principle which I pray may daily acquire strength in you. In seeking the growth of vital piety, you will experience an increase of its attendant blessings. Rest not, therefore, in your present attainments, but endeavor to acquire more and more of the character of a real disciple of Jesus Christ. Consider every discovery or attainment in the Christian life which either of you make as an addition to your common stock of imperishable good; and partake of it together, as those who have no interest separate from each other in anything. This is to live together "as heirs of the grace of life." (1 Pet. 3:7.) Let this "growing in grace," therefore, be a subject of frequent and earnest prayer to GOD for yourselves and for each other, that you may pass your days together as both redeemed by the same Savior, sanctified by the same Spirit, aiming at the same end, and hoping at last to meet in the same heaven. Thus, instead of being snares to each other, you will proceed through life blessing and being blessed, by administering tender admonitions when you see each other remiss, encouragements when disheartened, and consolations when depressed.

CHAPTER IV

Effects of Christian Piety on a Household –
Advantages of Order in a Family. –
The Family of Eusebius. –
The Unhappiness of an Irreligious Couple.

I have not forgotten what was hinted in the beginning of this address: namely, that one consequence of your union is the establishment of a household; and that hereby a power is put into your hands of contributing something to the formation of public manners. I trust that you are not willing to overlook this circumstance.

There is one duty in particular which the spirit of piety will dictate to you—namely, *the consecration of your house by the daily returns of family worship.* Let there be an altar in your house inscribed with the adorable name of your Creator. Here let the master be daily found, presenting, as the minister of GOD, the offering of prayer and praise. The religious care of a family seems to be spoken of as a certain effect of real piety in that account which GOD gives of Abraham: "I know *him,* that he will command his children and his household after him, and they shall keep the way of the Lord, to do justice and judgment." (Gen. 18:19).

By this acknowledgement of GOD a married pair evidence their reverence of his being; they draw down his blessing on their family; they diffuse a spirit of seriousness through it; and probably convey the seeds of piety in many other families. What objects are these to the formers of a new household! and how careful should they be to unite their respective powers in endeavoring to render that effectual which has such happy tendencies! Let not only the husband be ready to perform the duty in question, but the wife also. I have, indeed, doubted whether there were this concurrence in some houses where, however, the duty was not omitted. I have seen the master waiting for that part of the family which the mistress ought to have seen to be ready to attend him at the hour of prayer. Here is an impediment to family religion, proceeding from something defective in her to whom the internal affairs of a family are principally committed. But I am obliged to confess that the irregularity in question has not always been entirely the woman's fault. The master has in some measure been chargeable with it, by not fixing a certain hour, or by appointing an inconvenient one, for the performance of this important duty.

This and many other errors you will avoid by digesting *a system of family government,* and determining to adhere to it—an expedient which you will find to be a source of numberless advantages, and much more necessary to personal and social happiness than at first may be conceived. Where there is order there are silence, facility, and energy.

Among the points to which order should extend, there is none of greater importance than the proper distribution of time. Have a fixed hour for rising, for devotion, and for meals. Let there be an appropriate portion of time for every office, and for the labors or recreations of every member of your family.

How pleasing in this respect is the house of *Eusebius!*[7] He has the happiness of having

---

[7] **Eusebius of Caesarea,** c. 263–339, called *Eusebius Pamphili,* became the Bishop of Caesarea, in Palestine, about the year 314. He flourished during the time of Constantine the Great and Constantius. His surname Pamphilus came from his relationship with Pamphilus the martyr. Eusebius, historian, exegete and polemicist is one of the more renowned Church Fathers.

a companion who, in her province, acts with him in the maintenance of a well-digested system of domestic government. There is an appointed hour for breakfast, after which, it being on the whole most convenient, all assemble to pay their devout acknowledgements to GOD for the mercies of the preceding night. After this every one withdraws to his respective employment. Some of them appear no more till the stated hour of evening worship arrives and gives all an opportunity of coming together again. This exhibition of order with which you are presented in the morning is but a specimen of what may be seen through the day. On the Sabbath you perceive the like regularity. After breakfast the family is assembled to prayers. They are enjoined to attend this service in the same dress in which they are to appear in the house of GOD, that the preparation of their persons may not be deferred to too late an hour, and that, instead of spending the last minute at the mirror, there may be a little time for reflection or private devotion previous to their attendance on public worship. All being thus ready, at a few minutes' notice they are easily collected; and they proceed, as a united and regular family, to the house of GOD.

You perceive nothing like distraction in this house. Everyone knows what he has to do. Nor is the *sound judgment* of the superintendents more conspicuous than the *happiness* of the members of this family. Indeed, order is to be recommended, from its tendency to render everyone comfortable. It was this excellence and happy tendency of order, exhibited on a large scale, that contributed very much to raise the royal visitor of Solomon to that high pitch of admiration in which she exclaimed, "Happy are thy men, happy are these thy servants, which stand and hear thy wisdom continually."[8] These words were the utterance of an admiration, occasioned, among other things by "seeing the meat of his table, and the sitting of his servants, and the attendance of his ministers."[9]

The hints which I have given to you are the result of observation; and give me leave to say that in the whole course of my observation there is nothing that has so frequently struck me as a cause of unhappiness to married people as the lack of religion. This defect, nearly or remotely, produces most of the miseries of a state which was designed for the happiness of the sexes.

The evil effects of disregarding GOD are seldom more shockingly exhibited than in the

---

[8] See 1 Kings 10:8. These are the words of the Queen of Sheba.
[9] 1 Kings 10:1-3.

history of an irreligious couple. Here, where the greatest temporal enjoyments might be found, there are frequently experienced the most exquisite of human miseries. *The fear of GOD* being missing, the union becomes a source of incessant woes. How can it be otherwise with those whose nature is depraved, and who, living without any acknowledgement of GOD, are under no superior influence to regulate their temper, and to prevent the violence to which ungoverned passions are subject? They become the tempters and punishers of each other. Offenses are given; and no principle existing that would lead them either to forgive injuries or suppress resentment, mutual offenses are freely multiplied, and the quantity of wretchedness increases to a dreadful amount. What wonder is it, then, to hear of dire distress in such a family?

But many of the evils proceeding from irreligion are concealed from the public eye. And were all the grief, the loathing, the hatred, the remorse, the apprehensions, which are experienced, as conspicuous as the actions to which they give birth, we should not even then have a complete view of the case. We must follow the guilty pair into the eternal world, if we would ascertain all the effects of their impiety. We must hear their reproaches. We must see them, who once exchanged vows of eternal tenderness, transformed into beings of the most hostile disposition toward each other, and meeting only to augment their mutual accusations. This is the dreadful end to which the history of an irreligious couple tends.

Mercy, however, sometimes interposes, to prevent this awful result of things. The offenders are commiserated, changed, and made happy. Light breaks in upon them, and they see at a glance, the source whence all their miseries are derived; namely, a disregard of GOD. They repent. They are forgiven. They are transformed; and are now no longer to be described "as hateful and hating one another."

Thus reconciled to GOD, and to each other, it becomes the business of their lives to repair the mischiefs which their irreligion has occasioned in the family. Their house has been polluted; it must now be dedicated to GOD. There, he must not only be occasionally worshiped, but honored at all times. Nothing contrary to his supreme will can any longer be permitted to continue there. Evils are not indeed so easily removed, as they are introduced: but their aim is right, and GOD is on their side: and when he favors a design, the greatest difficulties are overcome: "Valleys are exalted; mountains are leveled; the crooked is made straight, and the rough places are made plain." Things thus renovated, Religion introduces Peace, an heavenly guest; and the social endearments of a family, cemented by the fear and love of GOD, are experienced.

The next chapter shall introduce to you a religious pair, whose house afforded an exemplification of this happiness.

CHAPTER V

Evander and *Theodosia* were both the offspring of pious parents. Their union was a natural one. It had all the qualities which accompany an attachment founded not merely on similarity of religious views: it was such an affection as they could neither suppress nor direct to another object. But though their attachment was not produced by their religion, it was nourished by it. Whatever they saw in each other's person or temper to unite their hearts was heightened by the satisfaction they had in each other's piety, and the consequent prospect of spending a harmonious life, and a blessed eternity together.

Their hands were joined, and they entered on a state blessed with all the enjoyments which an unshackled affection could yield to minds seasoned with the benevolence and purity of Christianity. Their equal regard to GOD diminished not one enjoyment in which a fond couple could share, but was, on the contrary, an additional source of pleasure. They "delighted in GOD;" and they delighted in the society of each other.

Their unanimity, their visible though unstudied interchanges of kindness, had an assimilating influence on their family, and served to give considerable effects to that religious order which they had established. The invisible world being in a great measure habitually before them, they both, in their respective departments, attended to those who were under them, whether children or domestics, as having the charge of immortals.

Such was their behavior toward their children that it seemed as if training them for an *eternal* state was, in their view, the principal purpose for which Divine Providence gave them an offspring. And to this business they applied themselves with pleasure. They began *early* with the infusion of religious ideas into the minds of their children, wisely inculcating, at first, those great and simple principles which are the foundation of all religion. They aimed at nothing short of guiding their offspring to

Christ, that they might know him, and by the aid of the Holy Spirit yield their tender hearts to him. They conceived that one way to prevent the introduction of evil was to preoccupy the mind with that which is good; and it never once came into their thoughts that they should be blamed for enforcing a truth on children because they were too young to see all the bearings of that truth as clearly as their instructors did. They had none of the subtleties and refinements of skeptics in their method of education. They went to work in a straight-forward way; what they had learned they taught: they trusted they knew "the way of salvation," and they endeavored to lead their children in the same path.

Impressed with the infinite importance of this part of a parent's duty, they *took pains* in it. To conduct a business of such consequence in a desultory way was, in their opinion, but a smaller degree of that criminality which neglects it entirely. It therefore did not content them to inculcate religious ideas; they aimed, in dependence on GOD, to induce moral habits. The *genuine Christian* was the model they kept in their eye. To see this simple character in their children—to see them avowedly on the side of truth, yet free from all affectation; evidently desirous of living a useful life, yet neither vain nor obtrusive—was a hope they expected not to realize without great pains taken on their part.

51

They counted the cost, and determined to pay it. Hereby they hoped to obtain the divine blessing upon their endeavors. This they constantly prayed for, believing, from what they knew of the depravity of human nature, that without it their labors would fail of success.

But this pious care was not confined to their children; it extended to every member of their family. It began to operate silently at the very sight of a new domestic. Aware of the sordid ignorance in respect to religion prevalent in the families of the poorer class, and knowing that in their own house there were better opportunities of learning divine truth, they never employed a servant without feeling an anxious wish that he might know something more of GOD by coming among them than he knew before.

Thus honoring GOD, they were honored by him. Their family was not a society of starched formalists, distinguished by some unnatural peculiarity of dress or language; but, while they looked like the members of other families, they lived differently. They were taught to reverence the word and ordinances of GOD. They were taught that the blessing of GOD, and the favor of their common superiors, were to be expected in fulfilling the duties of their stations, and in the discharge of good offices toward each other. *Favoritism* was struck out of that system which the heads of the family adopted; everyone knew that impartial kindness was the law of the house.

Thus taught, they repaid their teachers by practicing the lessons in which they had been instructed. The house was the abode of regularity, industry, uprightness, and peace. It was not exempt, indeed, from human infirmities; yet it showed to what a degree of excellence the human character, under proper management, may be brought; and it produced social gratifications untasted where the cultivation of religious principle is neglected. Nor was it easy to mistake the source whence all the regularity and comfort of this abode proceeded—the genuine religion of Evander and Theodosia. Their authority, their instruction, and their example, accounted for all that distinguished this happy society.

They had the reward of seeing the fruit of their labors. That house over which they ruled in the fear of GOD was not exempt from the ordinary visitation of Providence. Like other houses, it was subject to the incursion of death; and at length the event took place, but not companied with its usual horrors. The trial was softened by the manner in which it was met, both by those who departed and those who were called to give them up, the former being enabled to die rejoicing in the truths of that gospel which had been inculcated in the family, and the latter to find a relief under the painful stroke which separated one friend from the other in the well-grounded hope of meeting again in a better world.

The person whom it pleased GOD, in his righteous dispensations, first to take from this family was one if its most important and most lovely members. It was Theodosia, the wife, the mother, the delightful companion of her husband, the nurse and instructress of his children, the discreet manager of his domestic affairs, whose unremitting attention banished confusion from the house, and whose sweetness of temper filled it with peace. I need not detail every particular of her last illness; an account of the concluding circumstances will be sufficient for my purpose.

Her disease was of a lingering kind—a circumstance of peculiar advantage for manifesting the influence of religion in death Evander approached her bedside one morning, as usual, to inquire how she had passed the night; to whom she replied in the following terms: "I should be glad for your sake, dear Evander, to be able to say, I have had a better night than usual. I know how such a report would gladden your heart; but I am not able to give such an account of myself. Indeed, I find myself going apace; and I had determined, before I had the pleasure of seeing you this morning, to endeavor, before my illness renders me any weaker, to gratify a wish which I have almost through life indulged. I have never felt much solicitude about the kind of death which I might finish my course; one thing only I have been desirous of, which is, that I might not leave the world without being able to make such a declaration of the mercies of GOD as might encourage those who are walking in his ways, and admonish those who are not." She was going to tell her husband what was the wish she desired to gratify, but was interrupted by perceiving the tide of grief suddenly rising in his breast. They grasped each other's hands, and some minutes were spent by them both in the silent indulgence of tears.

When this effusion had in some measure subsided, she began: "We have thought of this before; and I trust we shall both be sustained in this last conflict. To you, indeed, the hardest part of the trial is allotted. You love me; and therefore, unworthy as I am of such a regard, you will feel a loss. I have, indeed, something here for which I could think it worthwhile to live. It is you. It is my children. But there is One above for whom I can willingly leave you all, dear as you are to me. I hope to be with him. Unworthy as I am of the least of his mercies, I trust I may warrantably rejoice in him as the GOD of my salvation. I have endeavored to know him. He has not suffered me to live in a state of indifference toward him. Grace has taught me what I am, and what I lack. It has taught me to look for present and everlasting happiness in making the mediation of a crucified Savior the ground of my trust, and his example the pattern of my conduct; and that grace encourages me to hope for the forgiveness of my sins through his blood. In this hope of salvation through him, and the sense I have of my infinite obligations to the GOD of all grace, I rejoice in the prospect before me.

"I have a confidence in you that sets me at ease with respect to the care necessary to be taken of my dear children; but, above all, I am enabled to leave them with GOD. Thus have I little to lose, in comparison with what I have to gain, by leaving this world; but you, my dear Evander, have yet to maintain the Christian conflict. Be, however, of good cheer. GOD is all-sufficient.

"You have often encouraged me in my religious course; permit me to make my last recompense to you in kind. GOD, I know, will bless you. He will keep you amidst the snares of life, direct you in all the labors and difficulties of the family, and support you in the last hour, as he does me. Then shall we meet again. I do rejoice in this expectation. I take delight in the thought of seeing *you* again.

"I thank you for all your tenderness, care, and kindness; for all your admonitions, reproofs, and counsels; for all the condor with which you have interpreted my failings. I am thankful for the example you have been enabled to set me, and for the care you have taken of my soul. You have watched over me in this respect; and I trust that I shall have reason, as a creature designed for a future state, ever to bless GOD for bringing us together."

She meant to say more, but her affections weakened the power of utterance; and she, withal, saw it was too much at present for Evander. He would have replied, but the occasion allowed him no command of himself. He would have prayed, and fell on his knees by her bedside; but, stopping in the midst of the first sentence, he wept, and retired.

Religion, while it cherished all the sensibilities which adorn the man, opened resources to Evander, who was no stranger to the views, faith and dispositions which form the Christian. Reflection and prayer in his closet restored to him the power of supporting another interview with Theodosia. He rejoiced with her in the prospect of everlasting felicity. He thanked her for having so well filled up her station in life; and, kneeling down, he blessed the Father of mercies for having vouchsafed to them that knowledge of himself, the influence of which had hitherto sweetened their society, and now relieved them both, under the pain of separation.

When he had risen from his knees Theodosia expressed a desire that all the family might be admitted into her chamber when their minister, *Paternus,* should make his visit. "For," said she, "our family worship has been one of my greatest enjoyments. I should like to join once more with all my household in this act; and, if I leave it to another day, it may not be practicable." Not long after, the minister entered the room, to whom, after the customary inquiries were answered, the proposal of Theodosia was mentioned. He was pleased with it.

In a little time all were ready. Every domestic was admitted into the chamber. The servants were arranged at some distance from the bed, but in sight of Theodosia, who was raised by pillows, supported by two of her children. The minister began by reading a portion of the fourteenth chapter of St. John's Gospel, to which he added a few reflections, calculated to infuse into the minds of this little congregation a desire to "die the death of the righteous." They were preparing to conclude with a prayer, when they were desired by Theodosia still to keep their seats. "Sir," said she, addressing herself to the minister, "will you permit me to interrupt you for a few moments, while I declare, in the hearing of my family, my faith in that Redeemer who you have preached unto us?"

He desired her to proceed.

"The testimony of a dying woman," continued she, "ought to have some weight with those who hear it. I here, then, declare that nothing supports me in the prospect of eternity but faith in a crucified Savior. On him alone I depend for salvation. On the merits of my Redeemer I ground all my hope of future happiness. And this I declare in the presence of my husband, children, and servants that they may remember that what I professed through life I rejoiced in death. Blessed Redeemer, accept my grateful acknowledgements of that love which led thee to die for me; and fit me to enter that society of glorified saints, who to eternity shall ascribe their salvation to 'Him who loved us, and washed us from our sins in his own blood.' Lord, I wait for thy salvation."

The minister then kneeled down and prayed; and thus concluded the last act of family devotion in which Theodosia joined. He then retired. The servants were preparing to withdraw, but were desired to stay. Theodosia thought that an admonition from her, in present circumstances, might impress their minds, and be long remembered. She was unwilling that the opportunity should be lost; but there was a native modesty in her, which always led her to make toward her point by delicate approaches. She chose, therefore, to cover her intention, which she did by calling first one and then another of her servants to her bedside, and making those kind inquiries about their health which were natural, as her illness had prevented her seeing them for some time. When she had thus gone round with her inquiries, she began to speak of her own case. She told them of her supports, of the goodness of GOD, and the blessedness of religion. She admonished them in the most affectionate terms not to neglect religion, nor to be inattentive to the instructions of their affectionate minister, to whose zeal, humility, and benevolence she bore witness. She encouraged them to seek the kingdom of GOD, by referring them to that composure which they now saw in her, who knew not whether she had a day to live. "Thus peaceful," said she, "will you be in the last hour, if you make it the main business of life to know and serve GOD. We may not all meet together again here; but be followers of Christ, and we shall meet around his throne in heaven."

To this tender address none of them were able to make any reply. With respectful and affectionate silence some of them approached to kiss her hand. Others were obliged to quit the room immediately, in order to give vent to their feelings. And all gave proof of having heard her with the deepest impression. Of the scene which followed no description shall be attempted; it being impossible for me to represent it justly. This was her giving a parting charge to her children.

The anguish endured on this occasion was unquestionably great; yet let it be remembered that, although the survivors of Theodosia suffered much in being obliged to separate from her, the supports of Christianity were felt. They knew that there was a possibility of their meeting again; and they derived comfort from what they had been taught—namely, that a far more happy interview awaited them, if they followed those "who, through faith and patience, inherit the promises."

These are the felicities of married life, where Christian piety is combined with natural attachment. In such instances we see something of Eden restored. How great and how lovely the contrast to the wretched family of an irreligious pair, is that, where the members live together in peace and love, delighting in GOD and in the society of each other, worshiping his name, regarding his word, attending regularly on his ordinances, discharging their several duties, bearing each other's burdens, and when the death makes a separation, quitting each other in the hope of being reunited in a better world, never to know a parting there!

Such was the family of Evander and Theodosia. Like them, may you rule your house in the fear of GOD. Thus will you be "lovely and pleasant in your lives, and in death not divided." You have entered into a state designed by Him who instituted it, (among other things) for your happiness. It is admirably calculated to answer such an end; but if it be perverted, you derive no advantage from it; be it recollected, however, that the blame in this case falls not on the institution, but on yourselves.

I have suggested a number of rules, because the end proposed requires the observance of rules. It is in this state, as in others, happiness is the reward of diligence. "In all labor there is profit," said the wisest of men. Let what has been recommended to you, therefore, not only obtain your approbation, or merely excite a wish that it may have its intended effect; but *make a business* of the duties to which you have been exhorted. It is now that rules are to be adopted: now, before the evils which they are designed to prevent, have made their appearance.—There is no difficulty in attending to them, now that your hearts are sincerely and warmly united. After a disgust taken, the rule may still seem good; but it may be felt to be impracticable.

Give yourselves to GOD, and to one another. Pray for grace to fulfill your mutual vows. Attend to the examples which the Holy Scriptures have assigned to each of you: and the more you study and apply them to the several occurrences of your lives, the more you will find, that they enjoin everything which has been recommended in the former part of this address, in order to preserve your first affections, and to cultivate goodness of temper. Thus will you be happy in yourselves, comforts to each other, patterns to your neighbors, and witnesses of the excellency of that holy estate in which the hands of the first human pair were joined by their Creator.

Advice
to
A New-Married Couple
in a
Letter to John Brashier, Esq.,

by the
Rev. Henry Venn, M.A.,
Author of "The Complete Duty of Man."

Yelling, January 23, 1777

My Dear Cousin: I regret the loss we had in not seeing you in your way to town; not merely as the visit would have given us so much pleasure, but as I should have an opportunity of talking very fully upon a subject of that first importance, and on which I can write but very imperfectly—I mean your settlement in life. The whole family joins with me in love to you both, and the most cordial wishes for your present and eternal welfare. This is what I am always wishing; and having, through the most adorable mercy and infinite condescension of GOD, been led into the way of peace myself, and to so much comfort every day as excites my astonishment, I would fain see all my fellow-sinners, and much more my friends and relations, brought into the same delightful enjoyment of life. I shall now, therefore, lay before you what I judge the sure and certain method of living a Christian life, profitable to men, and pleasing to GOD, in abundance of peace and hope, light and love, from heaven.

The first material point is *a conscientious waiting upon GOD in prayer;* not satisfied with bowing our knees, and beginning the day with devotion; but we must pray. I used long to exercise an idle, lukewarm way of praying, by which I got nothing, but deluded my own soul, as if it were a necessary consequence of my corruption, which all felt, and all deplored. But to pray without attention, or without importunity,—to pray with our hearts asleep, and worldly thoughts intruding, as guests of every character do into an inn,—is hypocrisy. If we are not grieved and afflicted at it, as our disease, and do not long for the Spirit's power, and confess our sinfulness, our religion is mere form. If we do lament it, we shall succeed; and, generally, our secret approaches to the throne of grace will be refreshing, animating, and the sweetest hours of our life.

When secret prayer is thus performed, one part of our earnest request will always be, that the worship of the family may be solemn and spiritual, affecting every member of it, and offered up with self-abasement from a company of vile sinners before a glorious GOD —a means of creating mutual affection and unfeigned good will throughout the day. I have had family worship ever since I kept house, but never, till within these five years, was concerned about conducting it as it ought to be performed. Not that anyone could discover irreverence in my manner, or that I had not some desire GOD should be honored, but my desire was exceedingly small; and I did intercede with GOD, that we might never meet together without the exercise of repentance, faith, hope, and love, and without such a manifestation of his presence as he has promised to "two or three" who are met together in his name.[10]

---

[10] This is of the utmost importance to those Christians who ardently desire to have communion with God in all their religious engagements. The following extracts from the memoirs of Boston, author of "The Fourfold State," are here added as a note to Mr. Venn's Letter, being remarkably to the point. "February 16, 1700. I have observed, this day and yesterday especially, that I was more remiss in family duties than in secret; and I think it is

When secret or family worship is thus performed, the blessing is to be confidently expected, in a recollected and watchful frame of mind amidst trials, and preparedness for them; in a jealousy of self-will, which is ever working; and in a fear of everything that savors of a sour, angry, hasty spirit, the bane of domestic felicity, and the great contradiction to the Christian temper. At noonday, as you are not engaged in business, you must contrive to find a season for retirement, to be with your GOD and Savior. Daniel and David did this in the midst of all their great employments and numerous cares. "Evening, and morning, and at noon, will I pray; and he shall hear my voice," (Psalm 55:17.) Probably you will say, I am sadly at a loss what to pray for at each time. My rule is this: When I do not pray at noon with Mrs. Venn, or if I do not find the spirit of prayer when alone, I read some psalm or some of St. Paul's epistles, and presently find matter suggested from those lively oracles, and generally the spirit of prayer too. And, when you find you cannot pray, rise from your knees, stand, or sit down, and ponder deeply on the state of your heart;

---

occasioned by remissness in preparation for them." "February 17. I have this day found my heart for family worship." "December 30, 1710. I spent a part of Monday morning in prayer, and by that exercise, and making conscience of preparing for family duties, I found myself bettered."

ask yourself some such questions as these: "Have I no sins to confess, no corruptions to lament? Have I no need of pardon, or of the Holy Ghost, that I can be so stupid, so hardhearted? Oh, what a sinful man! how sunk! how fallen! how unable to help myself!" "Lord, arise!" will follow; and, if it does not, this solemn consideration of your own vileness will be exceedingly profitable to your soul, and endear the name of a Savior, and convince you that you are saved through sovereign grace, abounding in GOD's Son.

At evening you must have a stated time for retirement and preparation for family worship; which I would entreat you always to have in the morning before breakfast, and at evening before supper, unless experience shall show that another hour is preferable. And never expect to prosper in your soul, if the food prepared for the body, or the setting out the table, bears any weight compared with the spiritual repast for the soul which family worship ought always to be, and regarded as one of the most solemn things which occur in the whole day.

Make a careful choice of serious servants, praying to GOD, who will, in such cases, direct and provide. And then, by careful observation of these rules, you will enjoy his peace, you will walk in his light, you will receive what he published his gospel to bestow, and be increasing with all the increase of GOD. Nothing higher, nothing greater, than this are you to expect. A family fearing GOD, working righteousness, obtaining promises, living in peace and love, is a picture of heaven in miniature. Such I pray your family may be.

There are two points more, of great moment—*company and public worship.* Nothing hurts the soul more than much acquaintance. The time is wasted; the attention is drawn off; an idle strain of conversation, even about religious subjects, is indulged; the spirit of the world creeps in, and a pleasure in entertaining and appearing just as those do who know not GOD. I believe more religious professors are injured by this error than any other. Be therefore deliberate and very discreet in the choice of your company. Always say to yourself, "Do I find either reproofs, or exhortations, or comfort, or instruction in the great things of GOD, from their company? Otherwise, what loss must I suffer, and how be thrown back, while I want every help to set me forward!"

With regard to preaching, never leave your own pastor, who preaches the gospel. For as rain, without which nothing can grow, can fall so often, and in such excess, as to prove no less hurtful than a drought, so it is common, very common, for religious persons to hear, and hear, and hear, till they are very little alone; are utter strangers to meditation; are as ignorant of the Scriptures, and the interpretation of them by the Holy Ghost, as those who hear only ignorant teachers. Once in the week, besides the Lord's Day, is generally sufficient. I had rather spend one hour with the dearest friend I have upon earth than hear him commended for days together. Private prayer, and mediation upon the blessed Word of GOD is spending our time with the beloved Jesus.[11]

Some would now be apt to say, "Must all this be done? Surely it is not needful." Judge from the shameful conduct of professors; from the complaints resounding, on every side, of masters against their domestics, and of servants against their superiors. Judge from the worldly compliances so common among those who hear Christ's ministers, and can scarcely, in anything else, be distinguished from natural men. Judge from the few who are fervent in love, active in zeal, judicious and animating in their discourse, clothed in the heavenly robes of humility and righteousness, whose words are as goads, are their whole deportment a pattern. Judge from the very great scarcity of such characters; and see how

---

[11] Weigh well these words in light of the multitudes in our day who listen to dozens of sermons each week on their computer or ipod. One of the grave dangers of listening too much to preaching is the danger of becoming a mere hearer of the word and not a doer (see James 1:22-25).

absolutely needful it is to do more than others, and to labor, in the way I have pointed out, for "that meat which endureth unto everlasting life." (John 6:27.) The general ruinous mistake of professing Christians is, that justification by faith, imputed righteousness, electing grace, and everlasting love, are to be believed, and extolled, and heard with great eagerness; and there alas! they stop. Not so the word of GOD; it teaches all these doctrines but as means of engaging our hope, establishing our faith, spiritualizing our affections, conquering the world, and making us long for the coming of the Lord, to whom we are dear as the bride to the bridegroom, and whose presence without a veil can alone satisfy us. Oh, the deplorable apostasy from a Christian spirit, while the doctrine of grace is maintained with zeal! I pray GOD ever to preserve us from such abuse, and make us long to be well-pleasing, in all our ways and doings, to him whom we call our Lord and our Redeemer.

I am so well recovered that next week I purpose beginning my usual course of work, which has been for more than a month suspended. I ride every day; and GOD has been pleased to recruit my strength. I was so weak as not to be able to pray with my family for near a fortnight. My son, by the help of Mr. Jenks, was my chaplain. You cannot think how I rejoice to hear that the minister so justly dear to us both is again able to lift up his voice and cry, "Behold the Lamb!" Oh, may he run, and all of us who are now in our last stage, as racers do, the swiftest; catch much of the fire from heaven before we enter, and be evidently transformed and fitted for that world of the redeemed.

If you and dear Mrs. Brashier are not dismayed at this long epistle, let us hear from you soon, and how you go on.

From you affectionate cousin,

H. Venn.

P.S. Mrs. Venn, as well as myself, hopes to have the pleasure of waiting upon you and my cousin in Yelling rectory, but shall first, most probably, see you at your own house in the spring. It is a noble promise to the Christian church, expressed rather darkly, "In that day shall there be upon the bells of the horses, Holiness unto the Lord. Yea, every pot in Jerusalem and in Judah shall be holiness unto the Lord of hosts." (Zech. 14:20,21.) The meaning is, The whole family shall be holy; and all that is done in it shall be done from a pure intention to please GOD. Such may your house be, and "the eyes of the Lord be upon it for good," from the beginning to the end of the year. Whatever comforts and blessings you enjoy together,—and may they be many,—still may you both be looking forward to that grand immortal life with the church triumphant, in the presence of the Lamb, for which your souls are forming. There I hope to meet you, and not yield to any one, in the whole armies of the saved, in acknowledging my marvelous deliverance freely bestowed on the vilest and most abominable of men. Then, how different from what we know now, our knowledge of ourselves and of our sin—of our Redeemer and his love! How different our feelings, our services, and our delight!

Could we leave our foolish dreaming
Of a fancied heaven below,
And see Jesus' glory beaming,
How our souls would long to go!

Extract From a Letter
to
Jonathan Scott, Esq.,
by the same author.

On the Study of the Bible

To secret prayer you will join devout study of the Bible, because it is our infallible guide, and the treasury of all truth necessary to salvation. But the riches laid up there are not to be found by proud or careless minds; none possess them till they dig for them as for silver, longing to know the will of GOD, that they may do it. To superficial readers of the Bible it presents little more than a great number of duties which must be performed, and sins which must be renounced, with insupportable pains on failure of obedience—passages of excellent use when believed, as they at once rouse the selfish soul of man to seek reconciliation with GOD and help from heaven, and sweep away every refuge of lies, under which love of sins leads us to take shelter. But earnest and devout readers of their Bible discover much more: they discover the tender heart of Christ, the efficacy of his blood to cleanse from all unrighteousness, and a variety of spiritual blessings, which are the present reward of being true-hearted in his service. I am at a loss for words to express how much solid knowledge, transforming your mind into the divine image, you will certainly gain by persevering in diligent prayer, year after year, for the true interpretation of GOD's blessed Word, that you may be made wise and holy. A pattern is plainly set before us in these memorable petitions. May they come from our hearts and ever dwell upon our tongues. "I am a stranger in the earth"—very soon to leave it; therefore its riches and honors cannot profit me —"hide not thy commandments from me," which will enrich me forever. "Open thou mine eyes, that I may behold wondrous things out of thy law." "Thy hands have made me, and fashioned me: give me understanding, that I may learn thy commandments." (Psalm 119:18,19,73). This method of reading the Bible must be continued through life, especially while the capital truths of the Bible are before our eyes. By this means we have an absolute security from abusing any part of the word of GOD. And those who dare despise persevering prayer to be taught by the Spirit of GOD what is contained in his holy word, as if they knew enough, fall into pernicious errors; wrest some passages of Scripture to contradict others; or grow violently zealous for doctrines, but very cold respecting that heavenly mind those doctrine are revealed to produce. Our profiting will then only appear, when, after the example of David and St. Paul, we pray from deep conviction that we cannot be properly affected with what we believe unless we are divinely taught, and that if any man thinketh that, without divine teaching, he knoweth anything, "he knoweth nothing yet as he ought to know." (1 Cor. 8:2.)

Select Poems

THE MARRIAGE VOW

Speak it not lightly! 'Tis a holy thing;
A bond enduring through long, distant years,
When joy o'er thine abode is hovering,
Or when thine eye is wet with bitterest tears,
Recorded by an angel's pen on high,
And must be questioned in eternity.

Speak it not lightly! Though the young and gay,
Are thronging round thee now, with tones of mirth;
Let not the holy promise of to-day
Fade like the clouds that with the morn have birth;
But ever bright and sacred may it be,
Stored in the treasure-cell of memory.

Speak it not lightly! Oh, beware, beware!
'Tis no vain promise, no unmeaning word:
Lo, men and angels list the faith ye swear,
And by the high and holy One 'tis heard.
Oh, then, kneel humbly at his altar now,
And pray for strength to keep your Marriage Vow.

WEDDING GIFTS

Young bride,—a wreath for thee!
Of sweet and gentle flowers;
For wedded love was pure and free
In Eden's happy bower.

Young bride, —a song for thee!
A song of joyous measure;
For thy cup of hope shall be
Filled with honeyed pleasure.

Young bride,—a tear for thee!
A tear in all thy gladness;
For thy young heart shall not see
Joy unmixed with sadness.

Young bride,—a smile for thee!
To shine away thy sorrow;
For Heaven is kind to-day, and we
Will hope as well to-morrow.

Young bride,—a prayer for thee!
That, all thy hopes possessing,
Thy soul may praise her God, and he
May crown thee with his blessing
-M.F. Tupper.

EPITHALAMIUM*

I saw two clouds at morning,
Tinged with the rising sun;
And in the dawn they floated on,
And mingled into one:
I thought that morning cloud was blest,
It moved so sweetly to the west.

I saw two summer currents
Flow smoothly to their meeting,
And join their course, with silent force,
In peace each other greeting:
Calm was their course through banks of green,
While dimpling eddies played between.

Such be your gentle motion,
Till life's last pulse shall beat;
Like summer's beam and summer's stream,
Float on, in joy, to meet
A calmer sea, where storms shall cease—
A purer sky, where all is peace.
                    -John G.C. Brainard

*(from Greek; *epi-* upon, and *thalamium* nuptial chamber, sometimes also spelled "epithalamion") specifically refers to a form of poem that is written for the bride. Or, specifically, written for the bride on the way to her marital chamber.

BRIDAL UNION

Ocean and land the globe divide;
Summer and winter share the year;
Darkness and light walk side by side;
And earth and heaven are always near.

Though each be good and fair alone,
And glorious in its time and place,
In all, when fitly paired, is shown
More of the Maker's power and grace.

Then may the union of young hearts,
So early and so well begun,
Like sea and shore, in all their parts
Appear as twain, but be as one.

Be it like summer — may they find
Bliss, beauty, hope, where'er they roam;
Be it like winter —when confined,
Peace, comfort, happiness at home.
-James Montgomery

HEAVENLY LOVE

They sin who tell us Love can die.
With life all other passions fly,
All others are but vanity.
In heaven Ambition can not dwell,
Nor Avarice in the vaults of hell;

Earthly these passions of the earth,
They perish where they have their birth;
But Love is indestructible.
Its holy flame forever burneth,
From heaven it came, to heaven returneth;
Too oft on earth a troubled guest,
At times deceived, at times oppressed,
It here is tried and purified,
Then hath in heaven its perfect rest:
It soweth here with toil and care,
But the harvest time of Love is there.
-Robert Southey

TRUE AFFECTION

Oh, there is one affection, which no strain
Of earth can ever darken, —when two find—
The softer and the manlier—that a chain
Of kindred taste has fastened mind to mind;
'Tis an attraction from all sense refined;
The good can only know it; 'tis not blind,
As love is unto baseness; its desire
Is but with hands entwined to lift our being higher.
-James G. Percival

HUMAN BLISS

There's a bliss beyond all that the minstrel has told,
When two, that are linked in one heavenly tie,
With heart never changing, and brow never cold,
Love on through all ills, and love on till they die.

One hour of passion so sacred is worth
Whole ages of heartless and wandering bliss;
And, oh, if there be an elysium[12] on earth,
It is this! —It is this!
-Edward Moore

MATRIMONY

There is an awe in mortal's joy,
A deep, mysterious fear,
Half of the heart will still employ,
As if we drew too near
To Eden's portal, and those fires
That bicker round in wavy spires,
Forbidding, to our frail desires,
What cost us once so dear.

We cower before th' heart-searching eye
In rapture as in pain;
Even wedded Love, till thou be nigh,
Dares not believe her gain:
Then in the air she fearless springs,
The breath of heaven beneath her wings,
And leaves her woodnote wild, and sings
A tuned and measured strain.

Ill fare the lay, though soft as dew
And free as air it fall,
That, with thine altar full in view,
Thy votaries would enthrall
To a foul dream, of heathen night,

---

[12] *elysium* - A place or condition of ideal happiness.

To Have and to Hold

Lifting her torch in Love's despite,
And scaring with base wildfire light
  The sacred nuptial hall.

Far other strains, far other fires,
  Our marriage offering grace;
Welcome all chaste and kind desires,
  With even matron pace
Approaching down the hallowed aisle!
Where should she seek Love's perfect smile,
But where your prayers were learned ere-while,
  In her own native place?

Where, but on his benignest brow,
  Who waits to bless you here?
Living, he owned no nuptial vow,
  No bower to Fancy dear;
Love's very self —for him no need
To nurse on earth the heavenly seed;
  Yet comfort in his eye we read
  For bridal joy and fear.

'Tis he who clasps the marriage band,
  And fits the spousal ring,
Then leaves ye kneeling, hand in hand,
  Out of his stores to bring
His Father's dearest blessing, shed
Of old on Isaac's nuptial bed,
Now on the board before ye spread
  Of our all-bounteous King.

All blessings of the breast and womb,
  Of heaven and earth beneath,
Of converse high and sacred home,
  Are yours in life and death.

To Have and to Hold

Only kneel on, nor turn away
From the pure shrine, where Christ to-day
Will store each flower, ye duteous lay,
For our eternal wreath.
-John Keble

To cheer thy sickness, watch thy health,
Partake, but never waste, thy wealth,
Or stand with smile unmurmuring by,
And lighten half thy poverty.
-Lord Byron.

EMPIRE OF WOMAN

Her might is gentleness; she winneth sway
By a soft words, and by a softer look;
Where she, the gentle, loving one, hath failed,
The proud or stern might never yet succeed.

Strength, power, and majesty belong to man;
They make the glory native to his life.
But sweetness is a woman's attribute;
By that she has reigned, and by that will reign.

There have been some who, with a mightier mind,
Have won dominion; but they never won
The dearer empire of the beautiful —
Sweet sovereigns of their natural loveliness.
-Friedrich Schiller.

SPEAK KINDLY

Speak kindly to her; little dost thou know
What utter wretchedness, what hopeless woe,
Hang on those bitter words, that stern reply,
The cold demeanor and reproving eye.
The death-steel pierces not with keener dart
Than unkind words in woman's trusting heart.

The very flowers that bend and meet,
In sweetening others, grow more sweet;
The clouds by day, the stars by night,
Inweave their floating locks of light;
The rainbow, Heaven's own forehead's braid,
Is but the embrace of sun and shade.
-Oliver Wendell Holmes

EQUALITY

They were so one, it never could be said
Which of them ruled, or which of them obeyed;
He ruled because she would obey, and she,
By him obeying, ruled as well as he.
There ne'er was known between them a dispute,
Save which the other's will should execute.

No jealousy their dawn of love o'ercast,
Nor blasted were their wedded days with strife,
Each season looked delightful, as it passed,
To the fond husband and the faithful wife.
-James Beattie

She is mine own;
And I am rich in having such a jewel,
As twenty seas, if all their sands were pearl,
The water nectar, and the rocks pure and gold.
-William Shakespeare

THE TRUE HEART'S ASPIRATIONS

I would be thine!
Oh, not to learn the anguish
Of being first a deity enshrined,
Then, when the fever-fit is passed, to languish,
Stripped of each grace that fancy round me twined!
Not such the lot I crave.

I would be thine!
Not in bright summer weather
A sunny atmosphere of joy to breathe,
But fear and tremble when the storm-clouds gather,
And shrink life's unrelenting doom beneath, —
Falling when needed most.

To Have and to Hold

I would be thine!
To lose all selfish feeling
In the sole thought of *thee,* far dearer one!
To study every look thy will revealing,
To make thy voice's ever-varying tone
The music of my heart.

I would be thine!
When sickness doth oppress thee
With love's unwearied vigilance to watch.
Waking—to soothe, to comfort, to caress thee;
Sleeping—to list in dread each sound to catch,
Thy slumbers that might break.

I would be thine!
When vexed by worldly crosses,
To cheer thee with affection's constant care;
To stay thee 'neath the burden of thy losses,
By showing thee how deeply thou art dear. —
Most so in thy distress.

I would be thine!
Gently and unreplying
To bear with thee, when chafed and spirit-worn,
The hasty word, the quick reproach denying,
But by the soft submission which is born
Of steadfast love alone.

I would be thine!
My world in thee to center,
With all its hopes, cares, fears, and loving thoughts;
No wish beyond the home where thou shouldst enter,
Ever anew to find thy presence brought,
My life's best joy.

To Have and to Hold

I would be thine!
Not passion's wild emotion
To show thee, fitful as the changing wind,
But, with a still, deep, fervent, life-devotion,
To be to thee the helpmeet God designed, —
For *this* would I be thine.

In the gay
And passionate hour of thy wedded hope,
When clouds have rainbows, and the earth has flowers,
Go in the glory of thy youth to him
Whose manly love has won thee. Let the home
To which he leads thee be the patient school
Of noble virtues. Let thy constant smile illume it.
When perchance the aching brow
Is sadly throbbing with the fever-stroke,
And solemn silence shrouds the room in which
Thy best-beloved lies sick,
be thou to him a ministering angel.
And when Death breaks from his ambush
on your happy path,
And bears his trophies to the spirit land,
May ye, with garments radiant as the sun,
Sit at the marriage supper of the Lamb!

SOLID GROUND BOOKLETS

SEEKING GOD BY PETER JEFFERY

"We have used Peter Jeffrey's *Seeking God* for many years to show unbelievers of all ages how to 'seek the Lord while He may be found'. It has proved most effective in special Sunday School classes, as a popular item on our tract rack with visitors and in believers' personal distribution to their friends. Seeking God shows you how to seek God, cautions you how NOT to seek God and encourages you as to why it all matters. Unlike so much fluff today, this is older, wiser, biblical counsel from a veteran 'obstetrician of souls.'" - **Steve Martin**, Pastor, Heritage Church, Fayetteville, GA

SECRETS OF HAPPY HOME LIFE BY J.R. MILLER

"This little volume is priceless! Miller rightly and forthrightly tells his readers that Christ is the secret of a happy home life; but he doesn't leave that as a nebulous concept. Miller breaks this truth into bite-sized pieces of spiritual instruction that bring soul nourishment on every page. The approach is truly pastoral. The memorable phrases teach practically, convict consistently, and comfort surely. This is a fine tool for the Holy Spirit to use in bringing the grace of Christ to the homes of believers." - **Bill Shishko**, Pastor

DUTIES OF CHURCH MEMBERS TO THEIR PASTORS BY J.A. JAMES
A PLEA TO PRAY FOR PASTORS BY GARDINER SPRING

This priceless booklet contains two pieces that ought to be read by every member of every church in the world. Many thousands of copies have already been used to open the eyes of those who owe a great debt to their pastors. Worth its weight in gold!

In the foreword to 'A Plea to Pray for Pastors,' Pastor John MacArthur writes, 'A Plea to Pray for Pastors' is excerpted from Gardiner's Spring excellent book, 'The Power of the Pulpit.' It is nearly 200 years old, but its message is as fresh and relevant as the day it was written. My own heart echoes this plea."

THE FEAR OF GOD BY JOHN MURRAY

"The fear of God could be nothing less than the soul of rectitude. It is the apprehension of God's glory that constrains the fear of his name. It is that same glory that commands our totality commitment to him, totality trust and obedience. The fear of God is but the reflex in our consciousness of the transcendent perfection which alone could warrant and demand the totality of our commitment in love and devotion."
- **Professor John Murray**

MORE SOLID GROUND BOOKLETS

FOR WHOM DID CHRIST DIE? BY JOHN MURRAY

"Of all the men I have known John Murray was the man I have judged to be most full of God. To see walking him about the campus set your heart beating faster and you hurried along to join with him, drawn by his love. Then you were careful what words you spoke when you were with him because of his holiness. He would take a class of students into the presence of God and preach his lectures with the deepest earnestness and clarity. He was a fearless Christian whose mind was bound captive to the Bible. Where the Bible went John Murray went and his heart was full of the atoning death of his Saviour as his only hope in life and death." - **Geoff Thomas**, Alfred Place Baptist Church, Aberystwyth, Wales

"One of the most difficult questions in the whole scheme of salvation is here simply answered by Professor Murray. He takes key Scripture texts and demonstrates the great success of the atonement leaving one to glory in the sovereign Redeemer of Calvary. This treatise changed my life thirty years ago. Today it remains at the top portion of my most significant reads." - **Robert B. Selph**, Pastor - Grace Baptist Church, Taylors, SC

DECISIONAL REGENERATION VS. DIVINE REGENERATION
BY JAMES E. ADAMS

"Being or becoming religious is not the same as being regenerate. That applies whatever the religion; even one that describes itself as 'evangelical.' As surely as everyone has to be born to live on earth, so everyone must be reborn to have heavenly eternal life; and no one can do either for himself. All life comes from God, and by way of gift. James Adams explains all this so clearly in these pages and also how the good news should be both preached and received." - **Hywel Jones**

"The error of 'decisional regeneration' has plagued the church for more than one hundred years. Dr. Adams, in this most excellent treatise, has exposed not only the error but so ably shown what the true meaning of biblical regeneration is from the Word of God. God grant that our generation may return to this truth as set forth in the Scriptures."
- **Robert G. den Dulk**

Call us at 205-443-0311
Visit us on-line at www.solid-ground-books.com